"Don't practice until you get it right. Practice until you can't get it wrong."

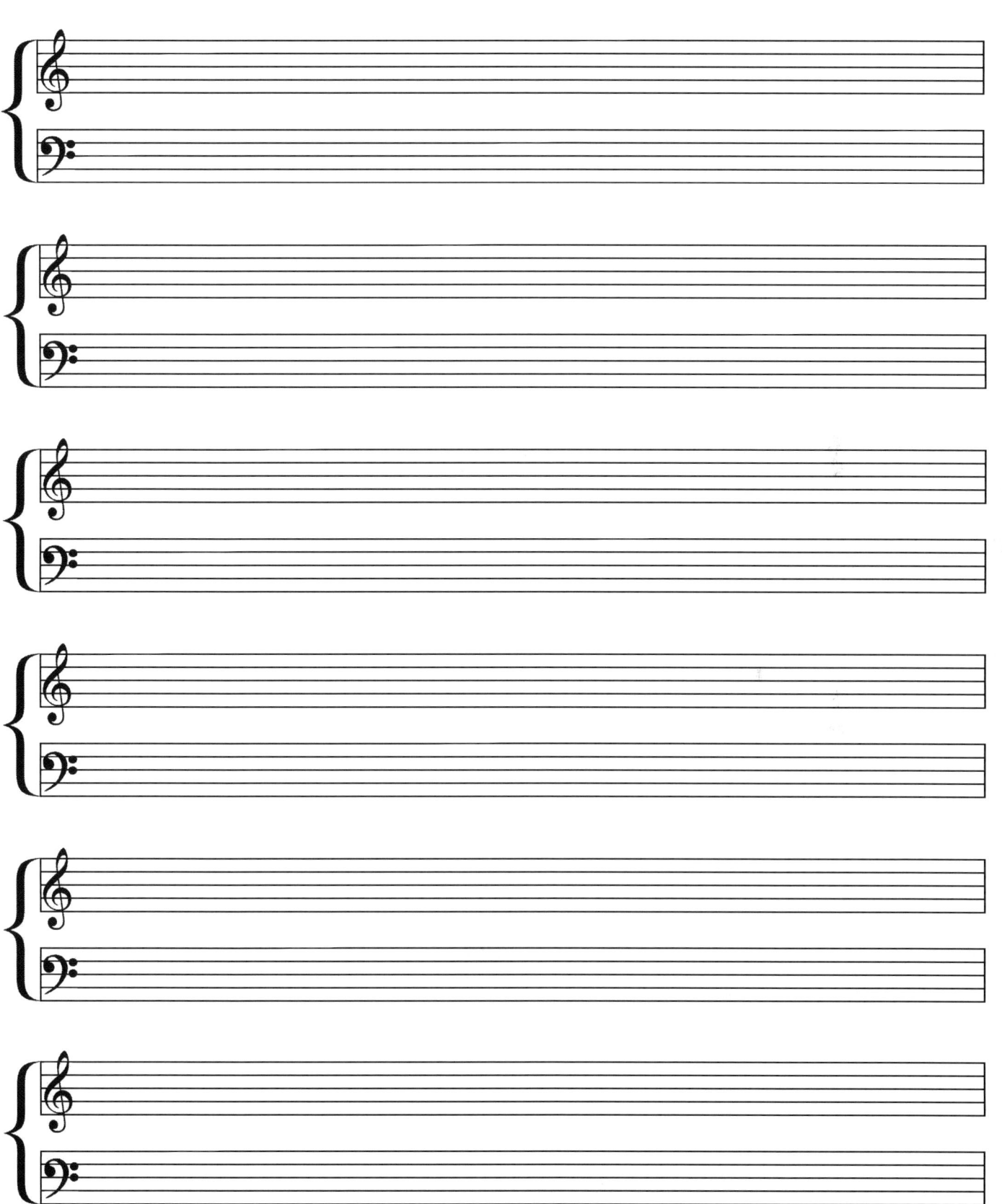

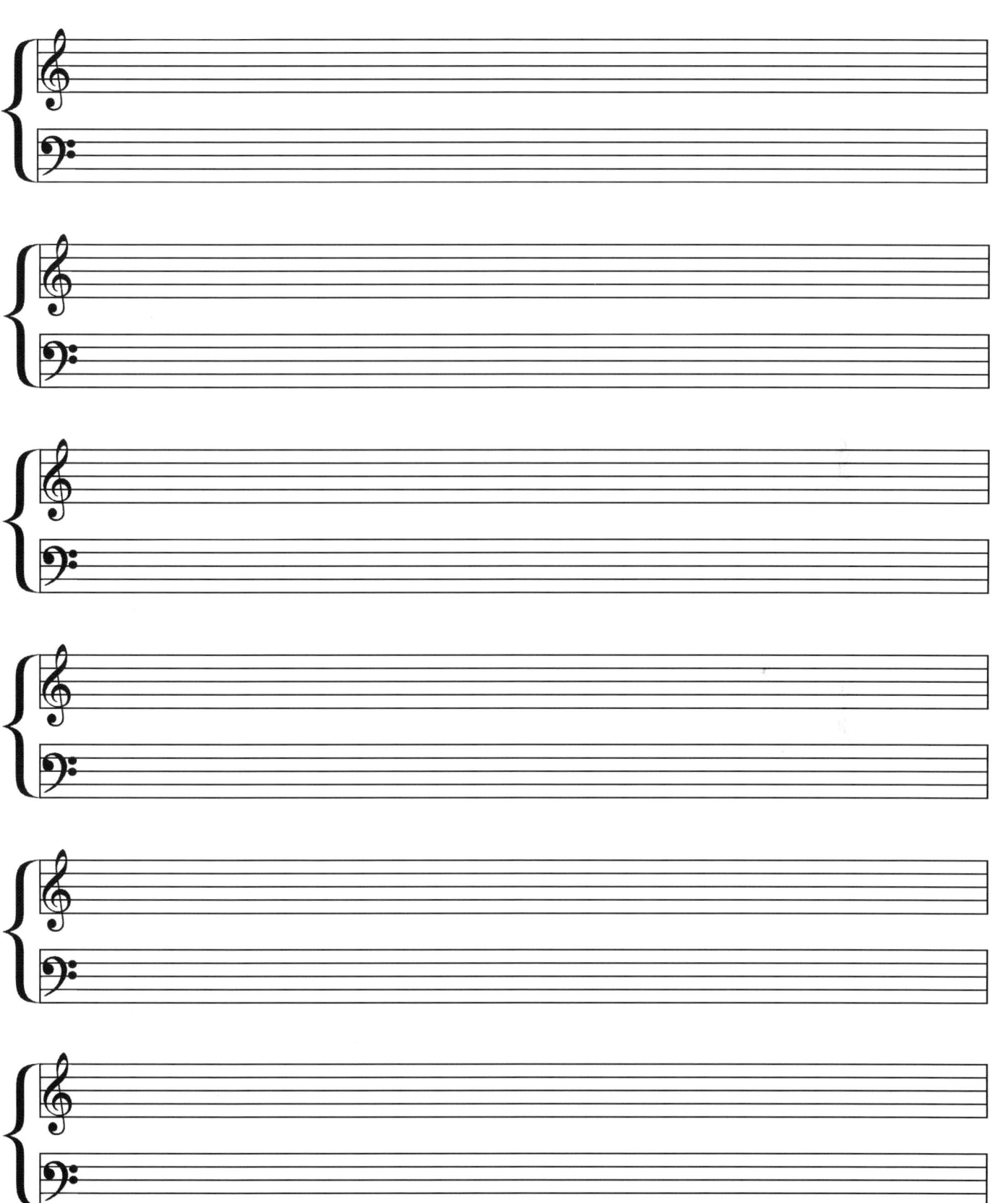

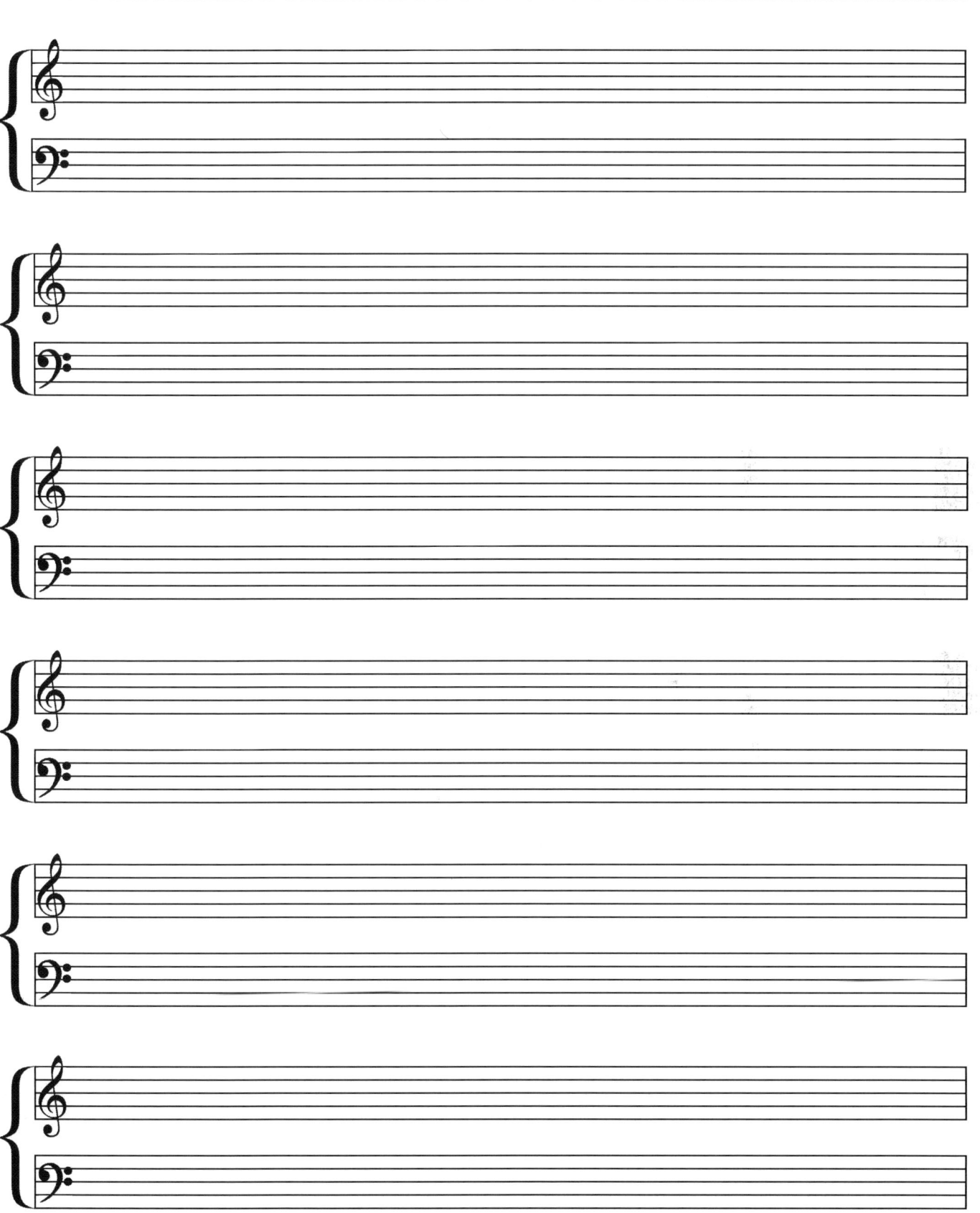

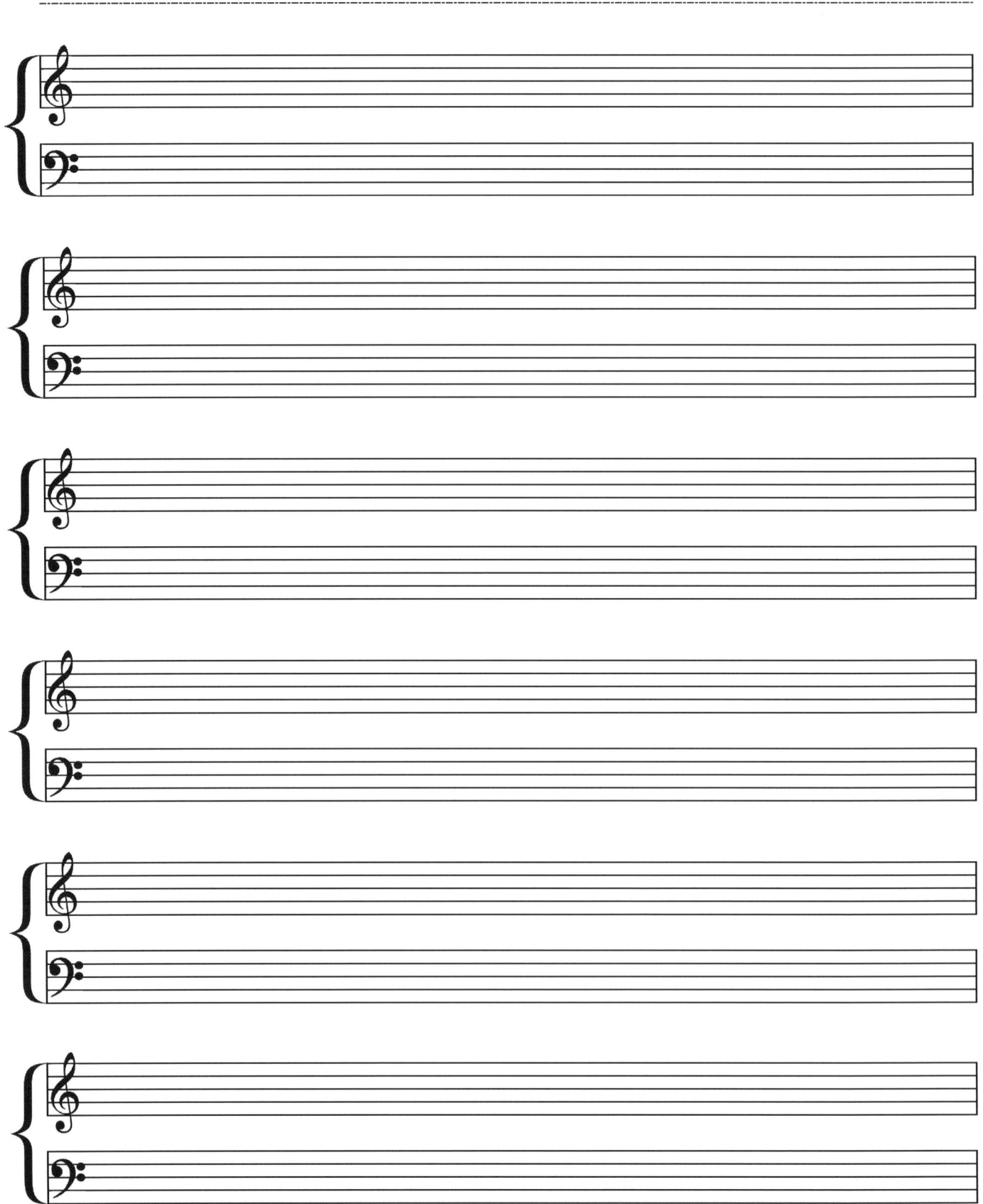

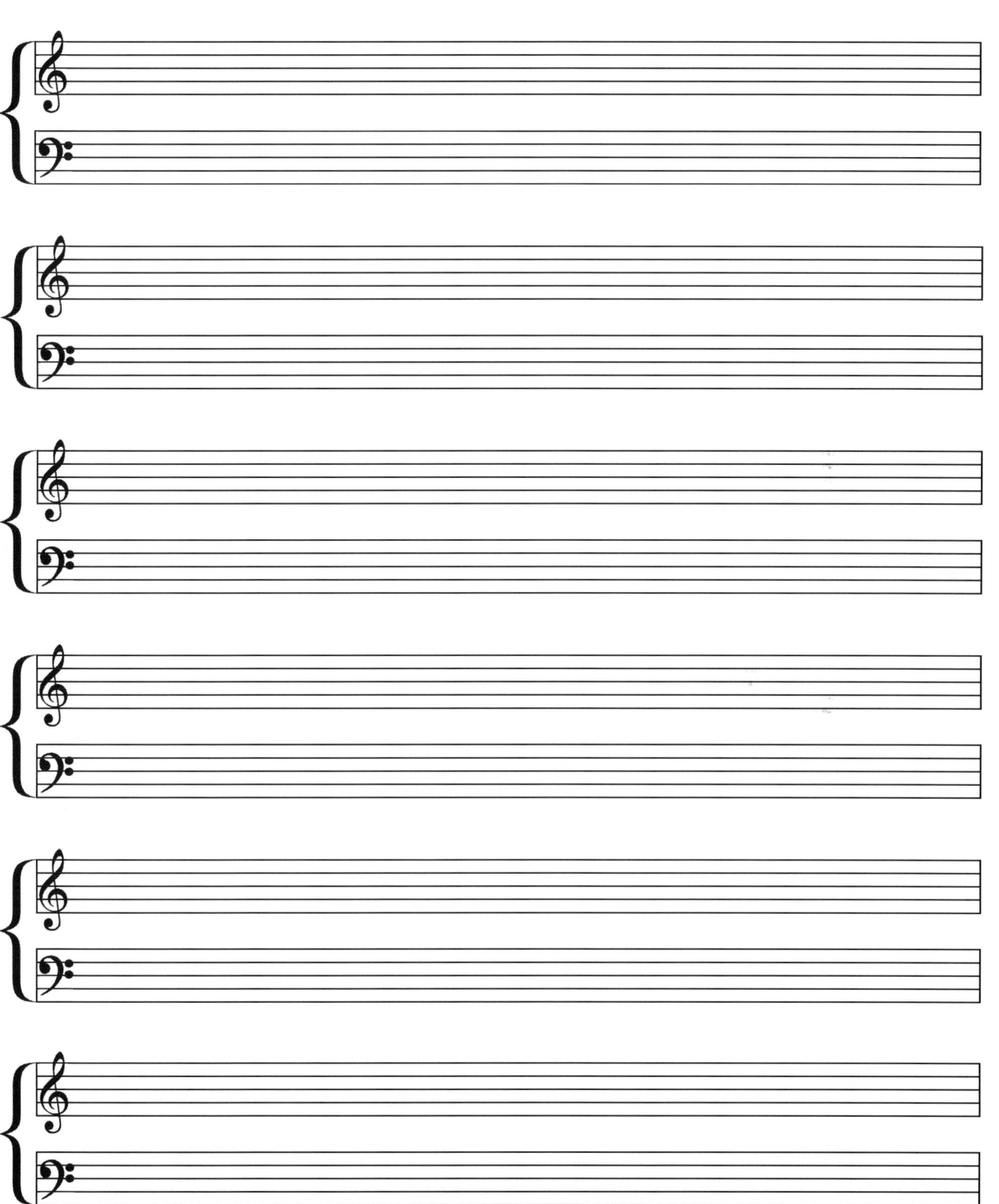

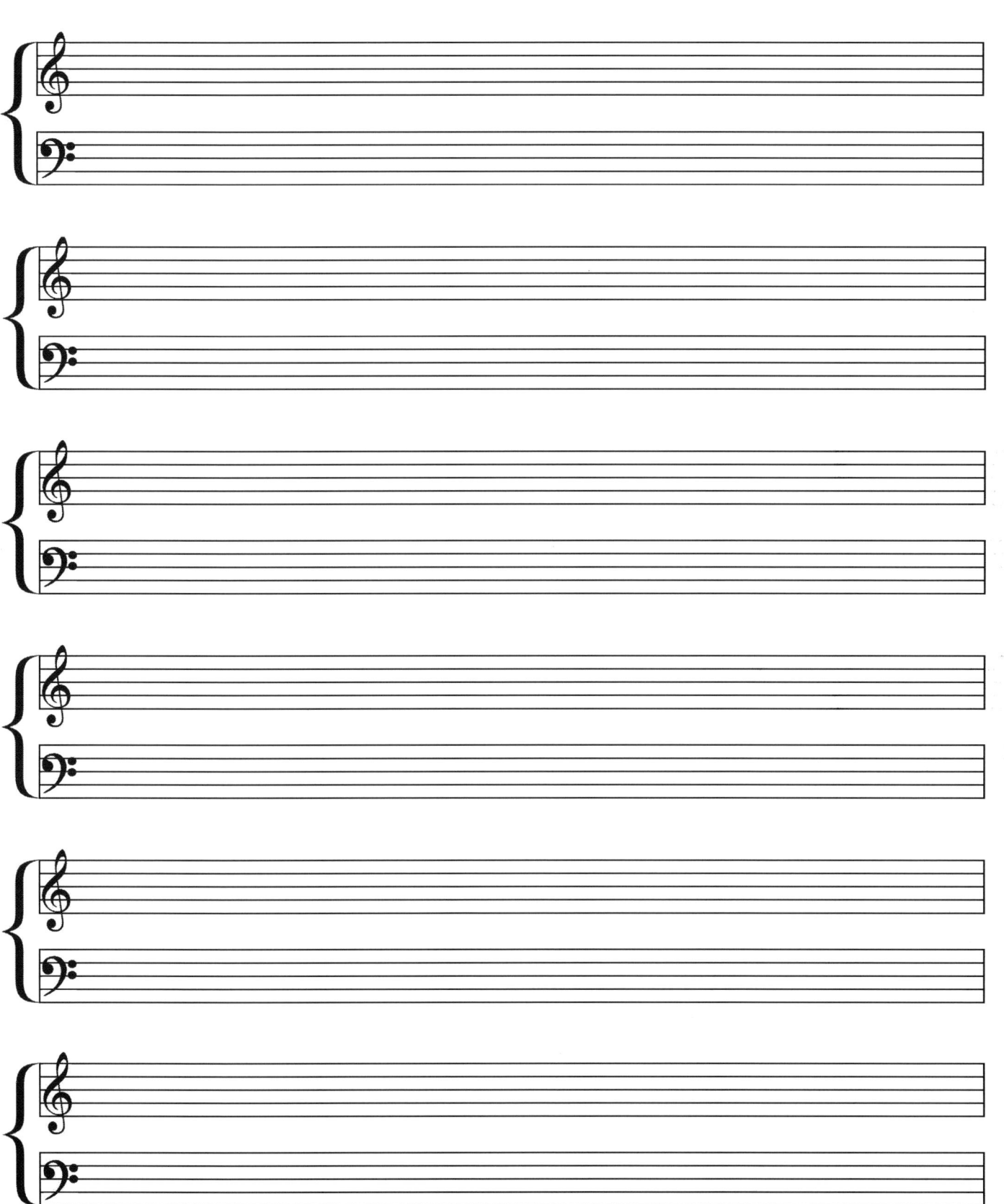

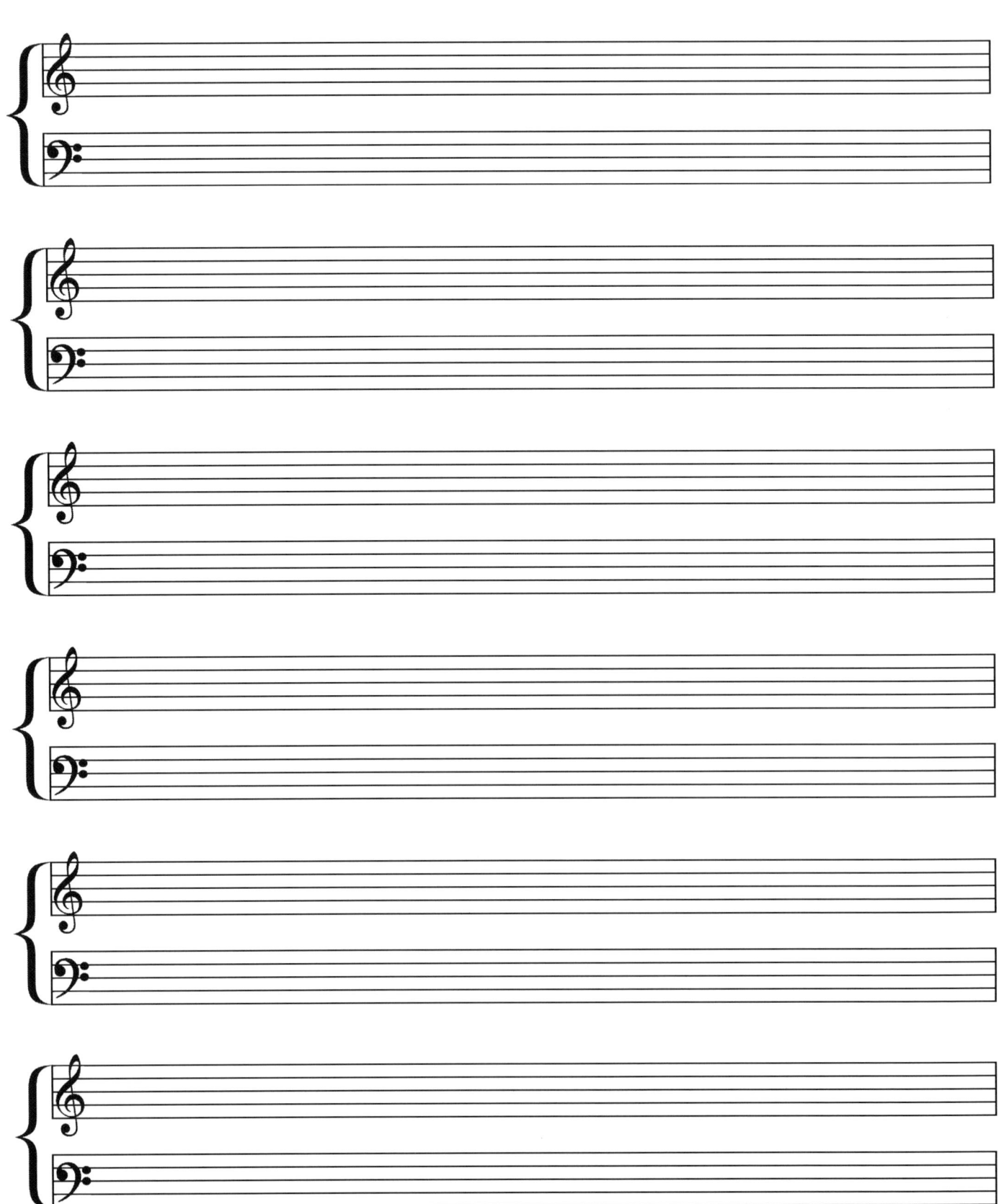

Music Theory Guide

Staff: A staff (plural staves) uses five parallel lines to notate the pitch aspect of music. Music is written on a staff consisting of five lines and four spaces. The lines and spaces are named after the first seven letters of the alphabet, namely, A B C D E F G.

Clef: A clef indicates which note names go on which lines (and spaces between the lines) on the staff. Clefs are written at the start of the staff. Treble clef designates the second line from the bottom as

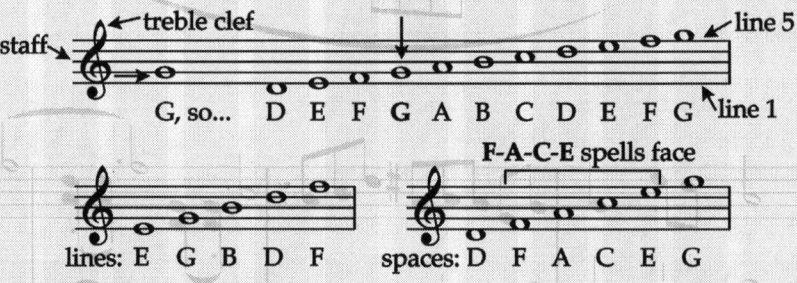

G. The lines in treble clef represent the pitches E, G, B, D, and F. The spaces are F, A, C, and E.

Bass clef designates the fourth line from the bottom as F. The lines in bass clef represent the pitches G, B, D, F, and A. The spaces are A, C, E, and G. This clef is used for the cello, euphonium, double bass, bass guitar, piano, bassoon, contrabassoon, trombone, baritone horn, tuba, and timpani. It is also used for the lowest notes of the horn, and for the baritone and bass voices.

A **Grand staff** is a treble clef staff and bass clef staff connected with a brace. Piano music uses a grand staff, along with instruments such as harp and marimba.

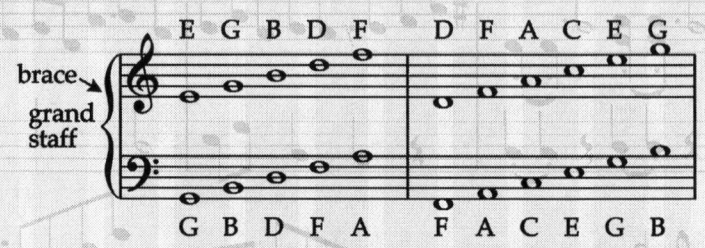

Sometimes vocal (choir) music is also notated using a grand staff. When playing the piano or harp, the upper staff is normally played with the right hand and the lower staff with the left hand. In music intended for the organ, a grand staff comprises three staves, one for each hand on the manuals and one for the feet on the pedalboard.

Ledger lines are small lines that extend the staff higher and lower. They can be used with any clef. Ledger lines belong to a single note; they never connect to ledger lines for surrounding notes.

C clefs: **Alto clef** is a C clef centered on the third line from the bottom, designating it as C. Parts for the viola (a string instrument in the violin family) almost always use alto clef.

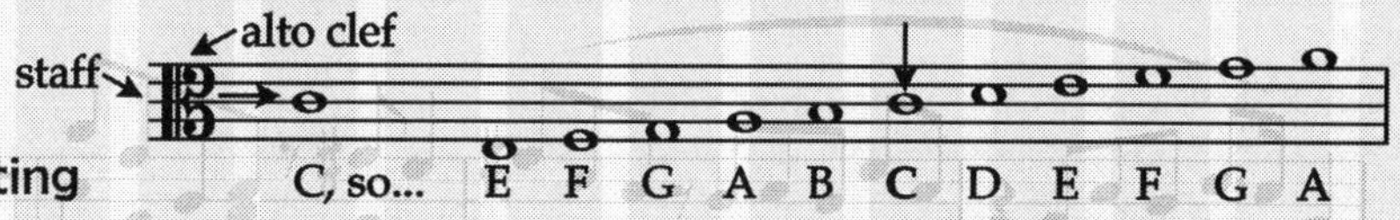

Tenor clef is a C clef centered on the fourth line from the bottom, designating it as C. Bassoon and trombone music occasionally uses tenor clef, although both instruments more commonly read bass clef.

RHYTHM

Rhythm is the element of "TIME" in music. When you tap your foot to the music, you are "keeping the beat" or following the structural rhythmic pulse of the music. There are several important aspects of rhythm:

DURATION: how long a sound (or silence) lasts.
TEMPO: the speed of the BEAT.
- **Largo** = "large" or labored (slow)
- **Adagio** = slow
- **Andante** = steady "walking" tempo
- **Moderato** = moderate
- **Allegro** = fast ("happy")
- **Presto** = very fast

⟵──────SLOWER   FASTER──────⟶

	Largo	*Adagio*	*Andante*	*Moderato*	*Allegro*	*Presto*
Beats per minute	40-65	66-75	76-107	108-119	120-167	168-208

These tempos are not specific—but RELATIVE to each other.

METER: Beats organized into recognizable/recurring accent patterns. Meter can be seen/felt through the standard patterns used by conductors.

DUPLE meter — a 2-pulse grouping
2/4 — STRONG weak — 1 2

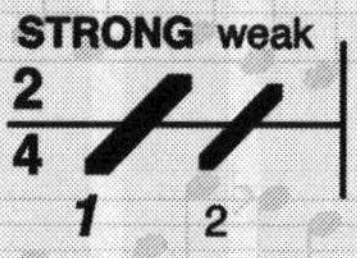

TRIPLE meter — a 3-pulse grouping
3/4 — STRONG weak weak — 1 2 3

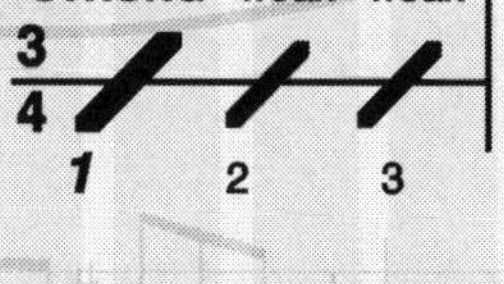

QUADRUPLE meter — a 4-pulse grouping
4/4 — STRONG weak Medium weak — 1 2 3 4

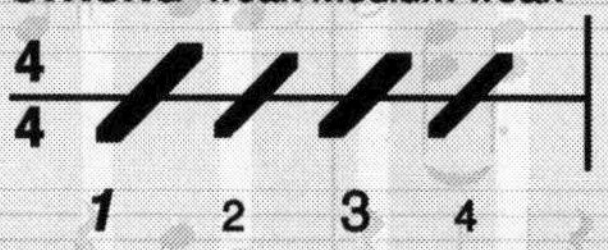

All musical aspects relating to the relative loudness (or quietness) of music fall under the general element of **DYNAMICS**.

The terms used to describe dynamic levels are often in Italian:

pianissimo [pp] = (very quiet)
piano [p] = (quiet)
mezzo-piano [mp] = (moderately quiet)
mezzo-forte [mf] = (moderately loud)
forte [f] = (loud)
fortissimo [ff] = (very loud)

Other basic terms relating to **Dynamics** are:

Crescendo: gradually getting LOUDER
Diminuendo (or decrescendo) : gradually getting QUIETER
Accent: "punching" or "leaning into" a note harder to temporarily emphasize it.

Duration is how long a note or rest is to be played. Notes and rests have fractional durations. A Half-note is half as long as a Whole-note, a Quarter-note is a quarter as long as a Whole-note and is also half as long as a Half-note, and so forth. Each duration will have its own symbol.

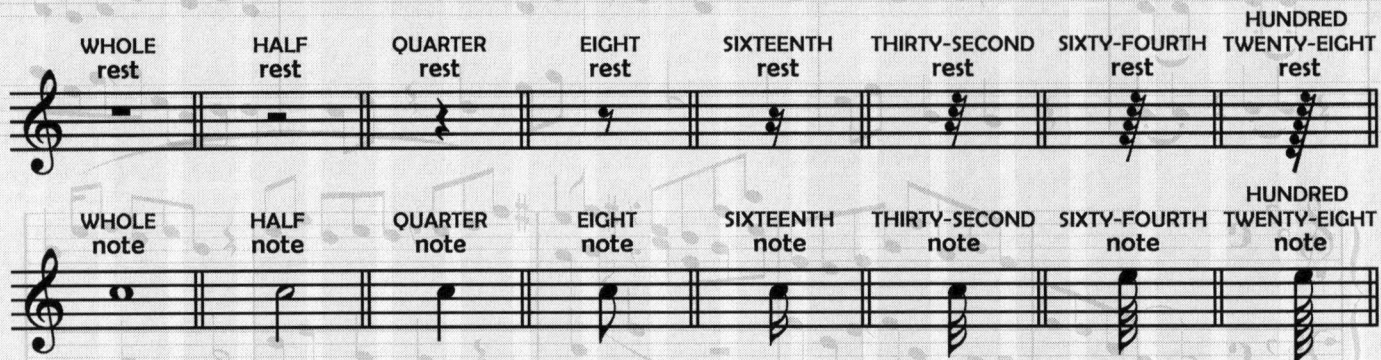

TIES may also be used to make the rhythmic duration of a note longer. The value of the second note in the TIE is added to the first. **RESTS ARE NEVER TIED.**

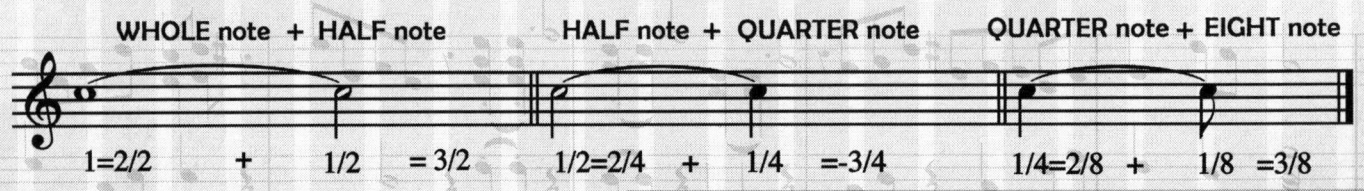

Key Signatures tell us what notes are sharp or flat in a scale. Any single Key Signature symbol will identify both a Major and Minor scale, for example C Major and A Minor have the same symbol.

Time Signatures tell us what the meter is and what note values comprise the beat. Time signatures are written as two numbers, with one number above the other.

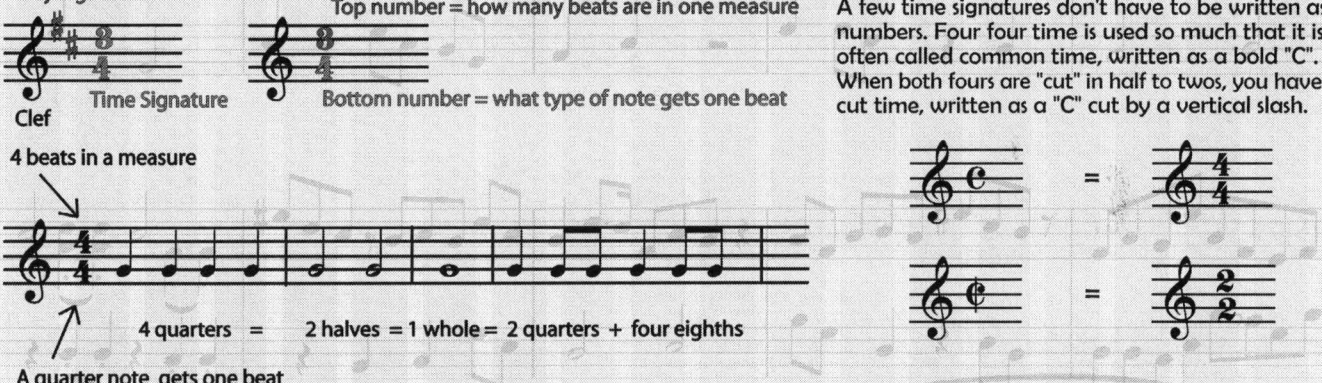

A few time signatures don't have to be written as numbers. Four four time is used so much that it is often called common time, written as a bold "C". When both fours are "cut" in half to twos, you have cut time, written as a "C" cut by a vertical slash.

An **Interval** is the pitch distance (high-low distance) between two notes.

Major and perfect quality intervals

match the notes of a major scale, starting from the first note of the scale up. Seconds, thirds, sixths, and sevenths can be major in quality, but never perfect. Unisons, fourths, fifths, and octaves can be perfect in quality, but never major.

Minor intervals are one half step smaller than major intervals, keeping the same letter names. Only intervals that can be major are able to become minor: seconds, thirds, sixths, and sevenths only.

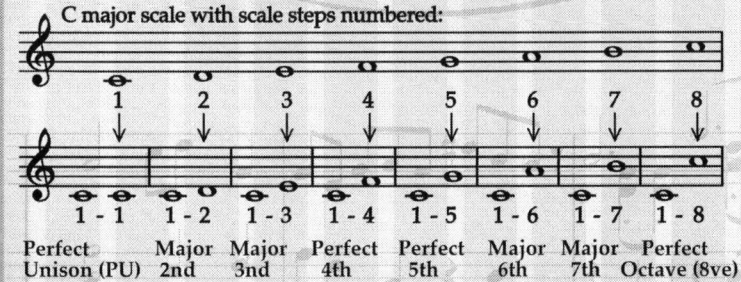

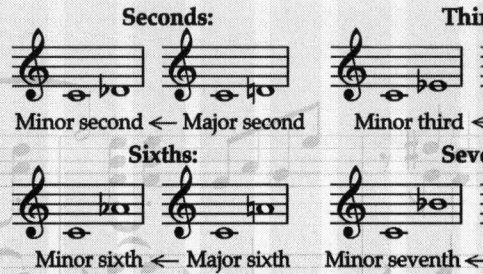

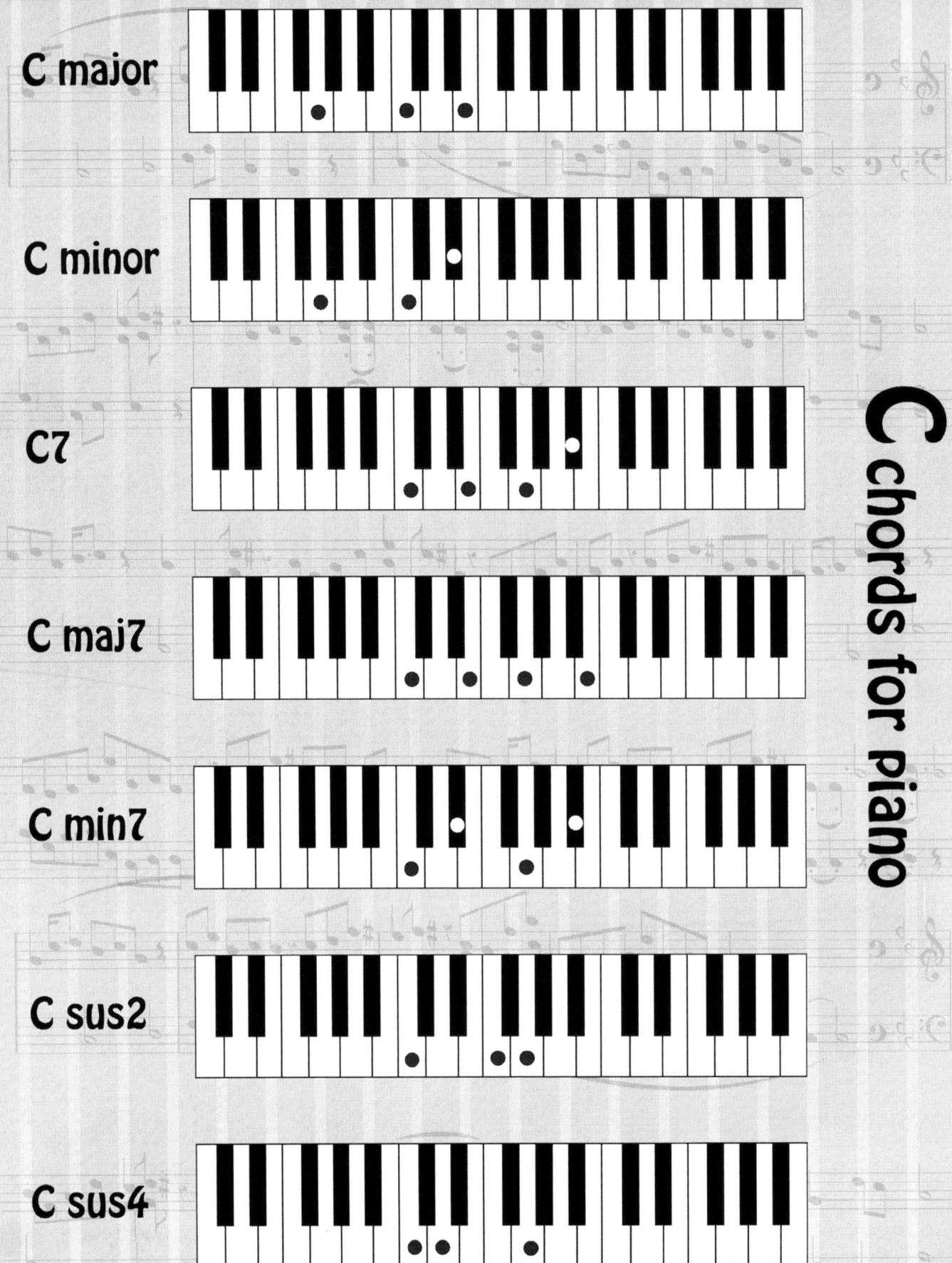

C#/Db chords for piano

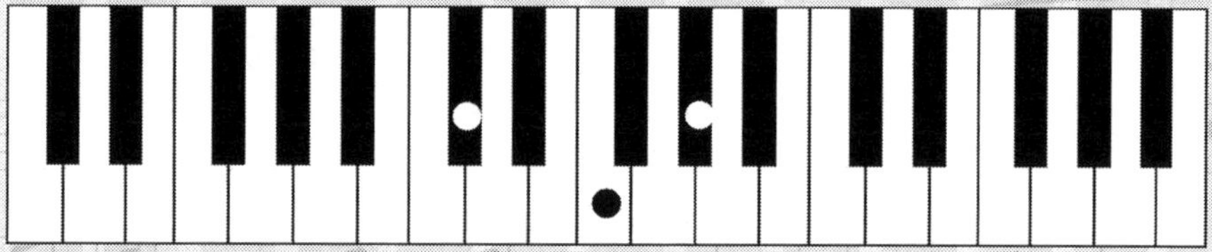

C#/Db major

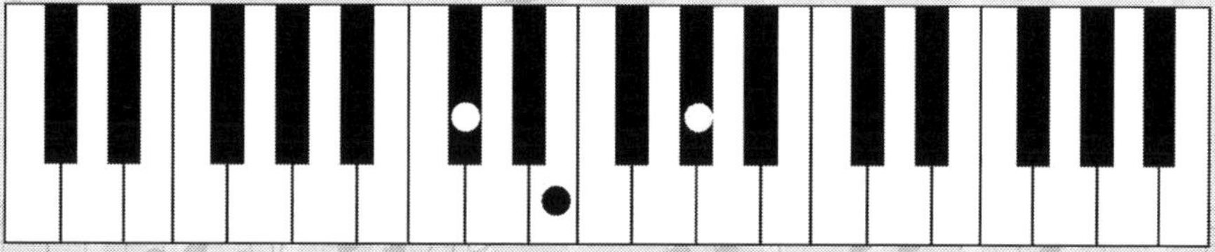

C#/Db minor

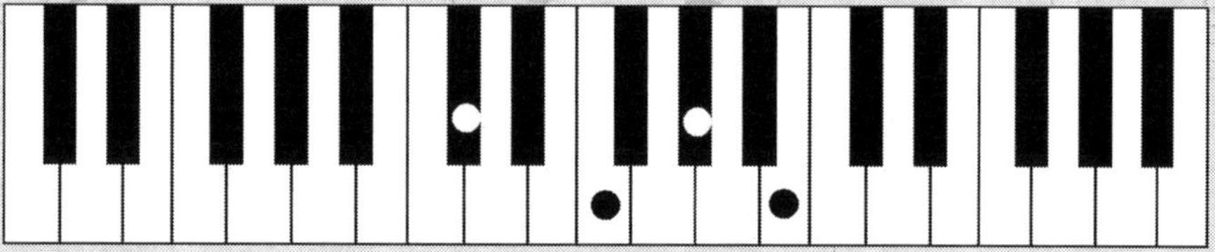

C#/Db 7

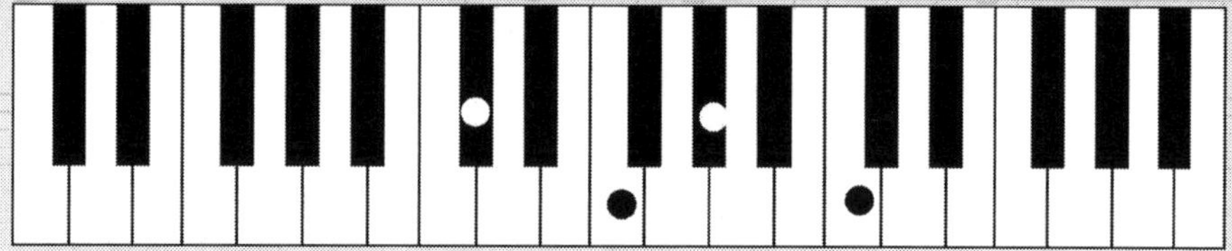

C#/Db maj7

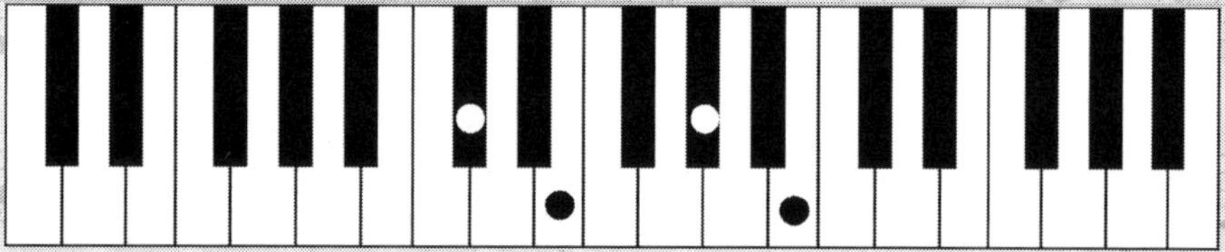

C#/Db min7

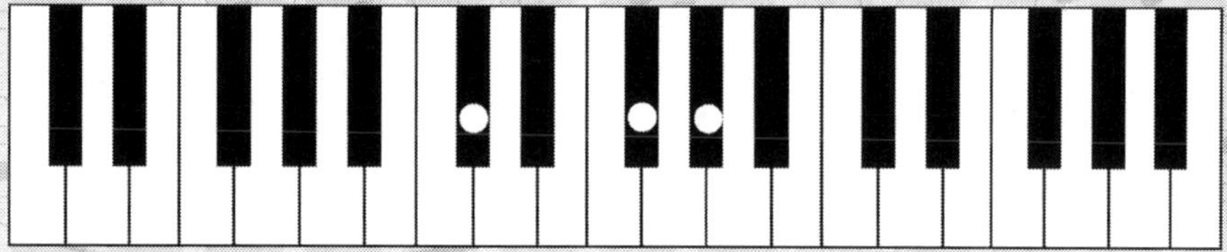

C#/Db sus4

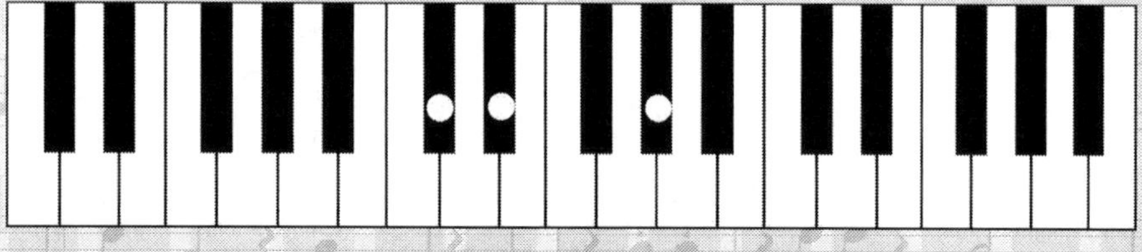

C#/Db sus2

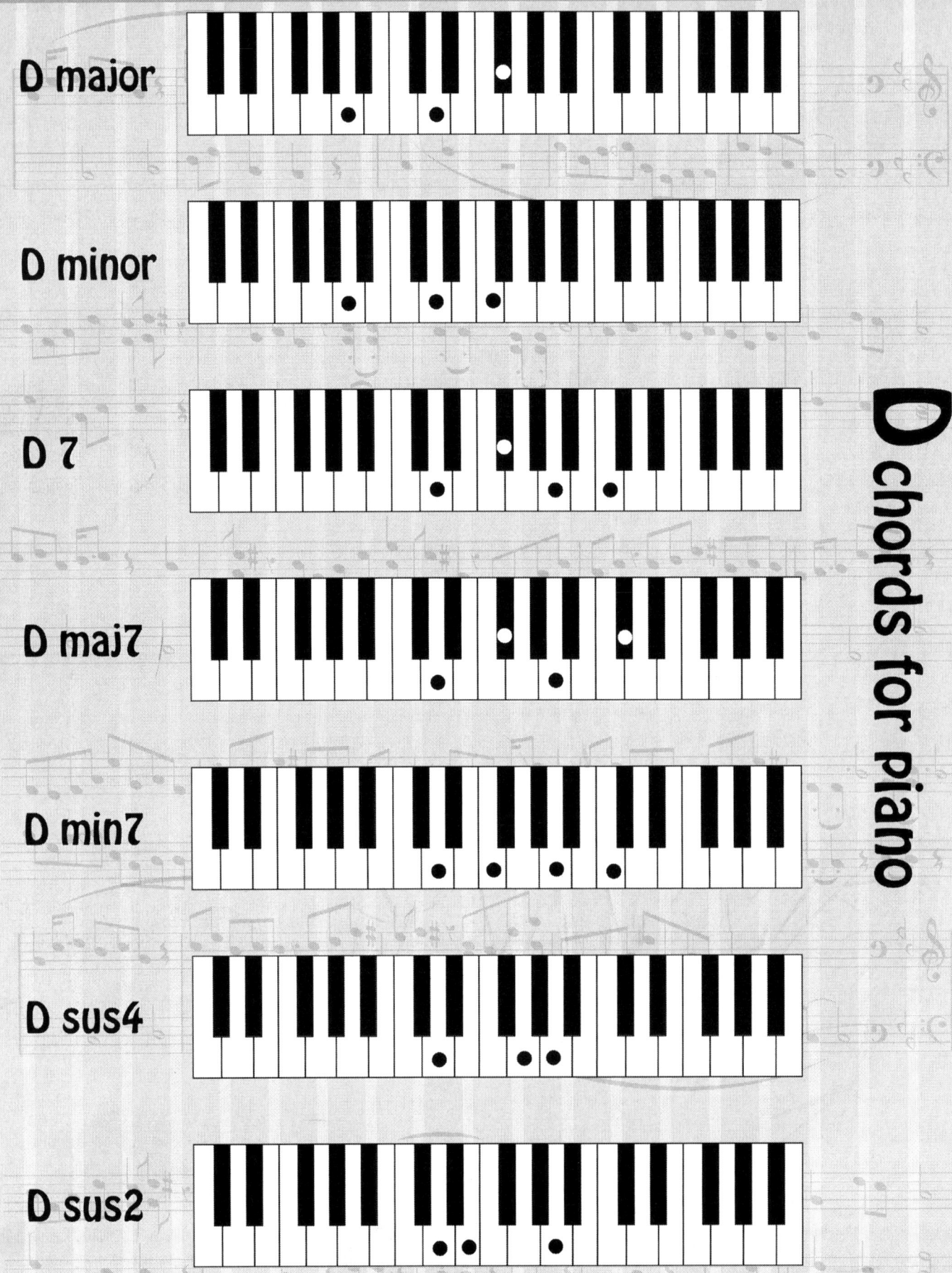

D#/Eb chords for piano

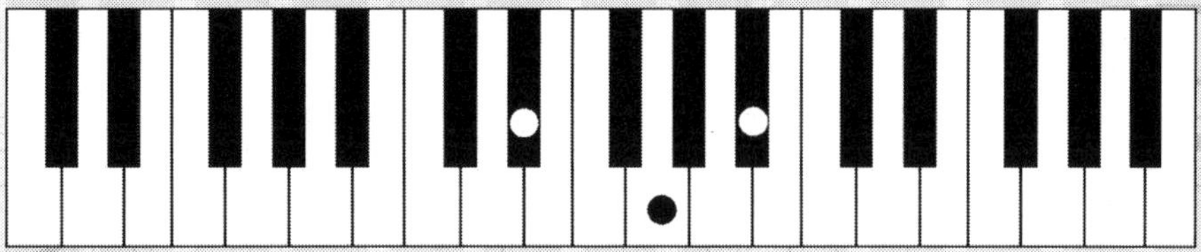

- D#/Eb major
- D#/Eb minor 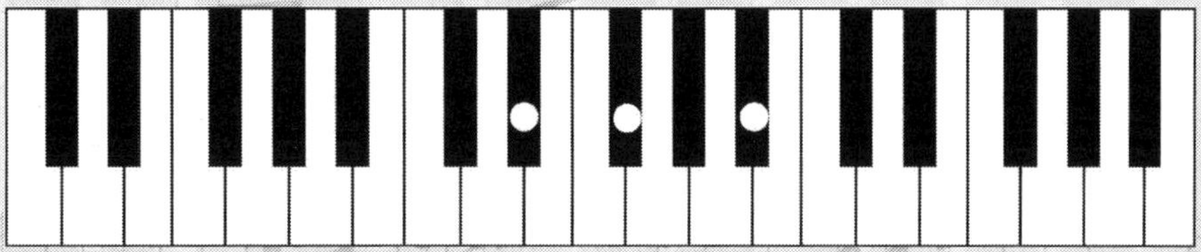
- D#/Eb 7 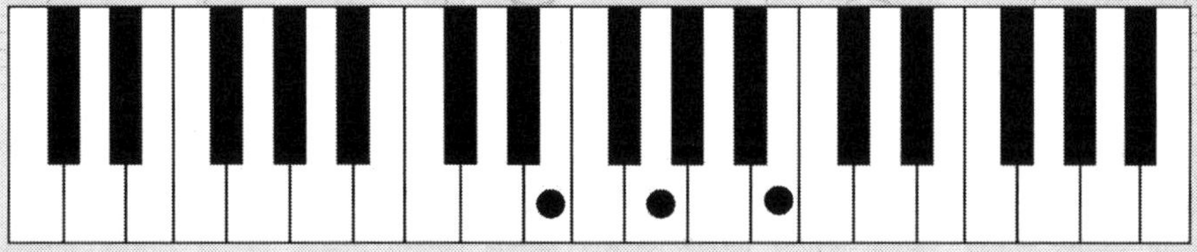
- D#/Eb maj7 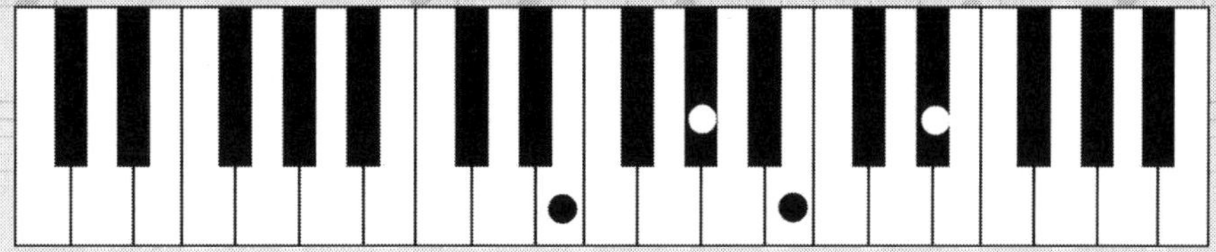
- D#/Eb min7 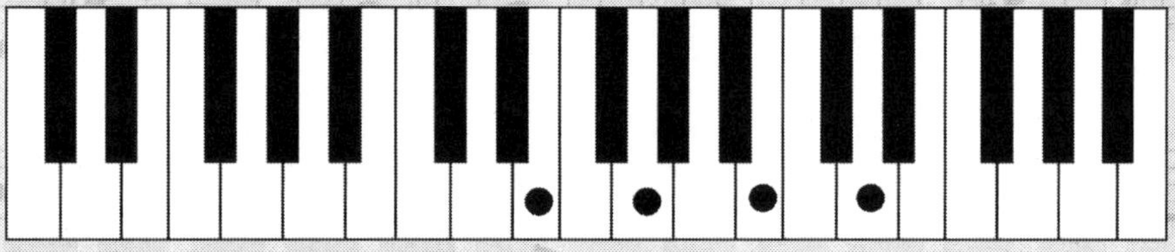
- D#/Eb sus4 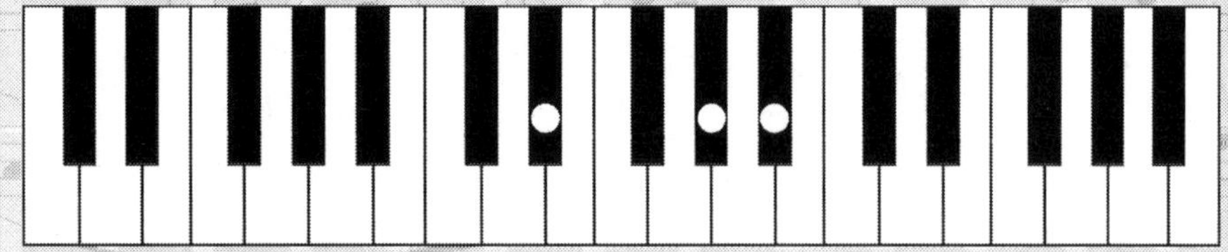
- D#/Eb sus2

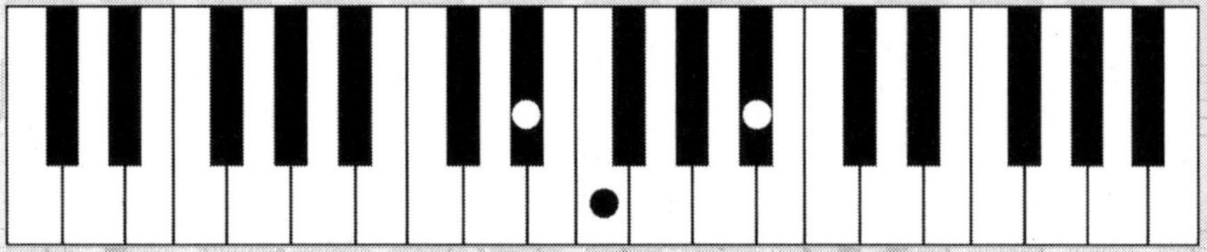

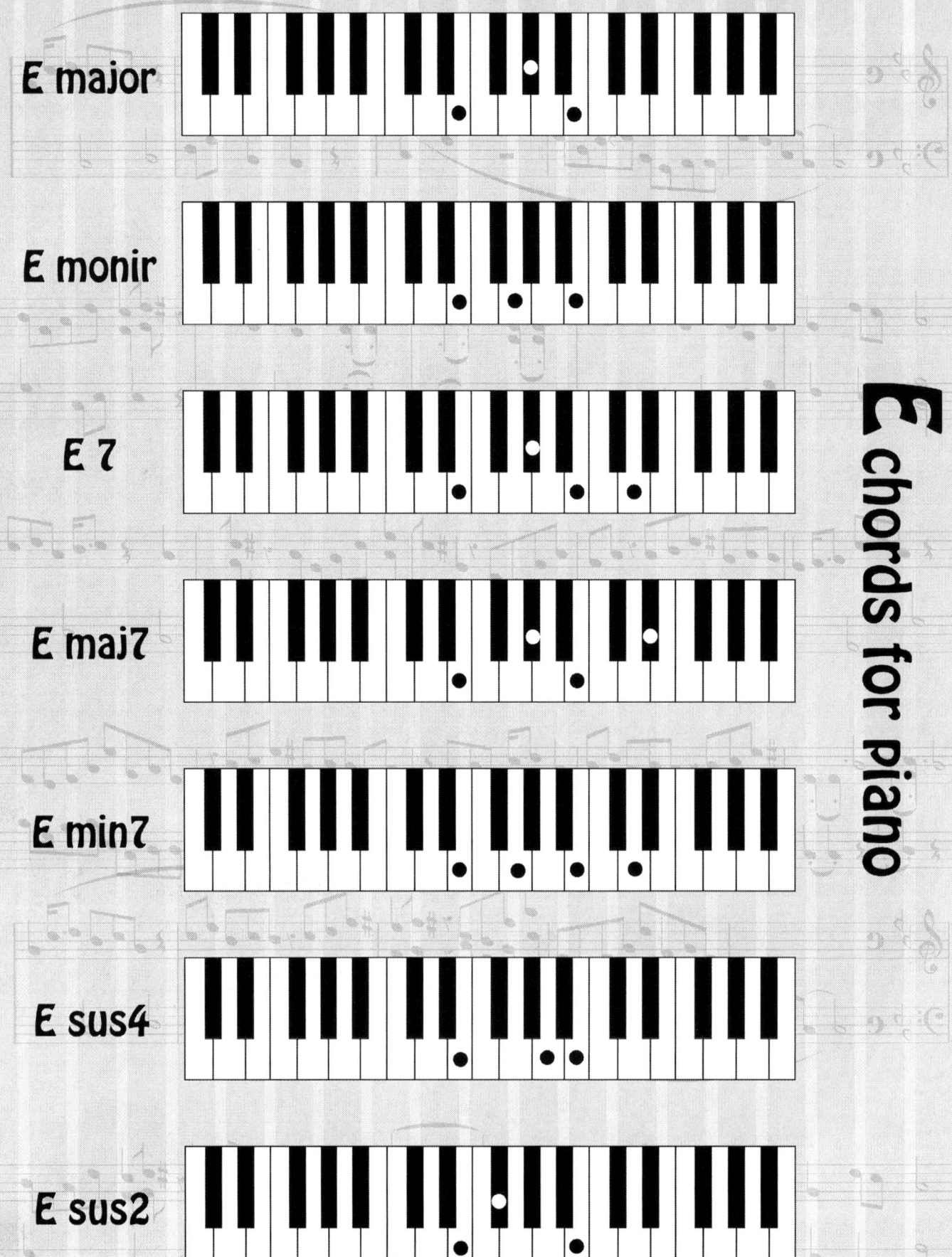

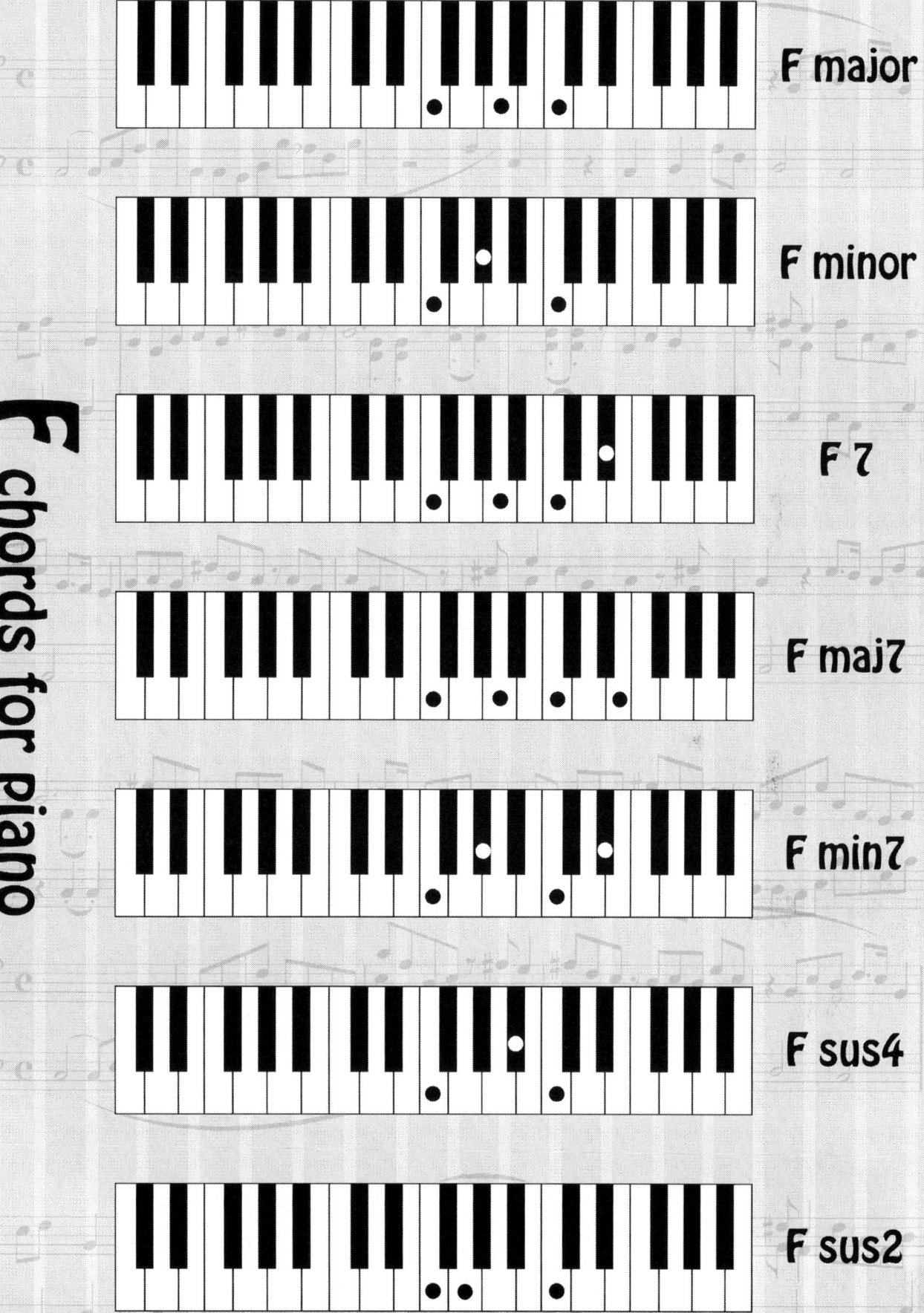

F#/Gb chords for piano

- F#/Gb major 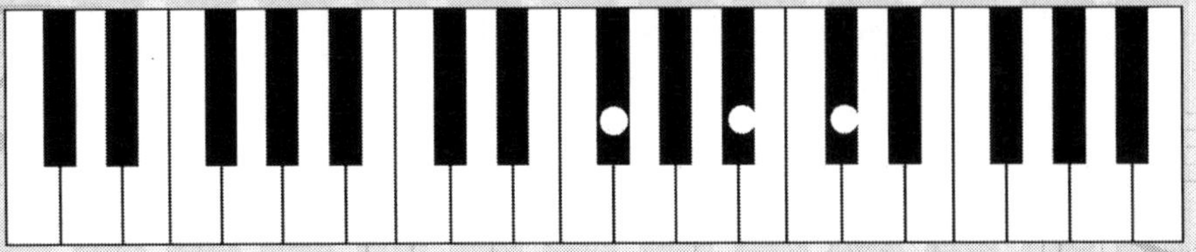
- F#/Gb minor 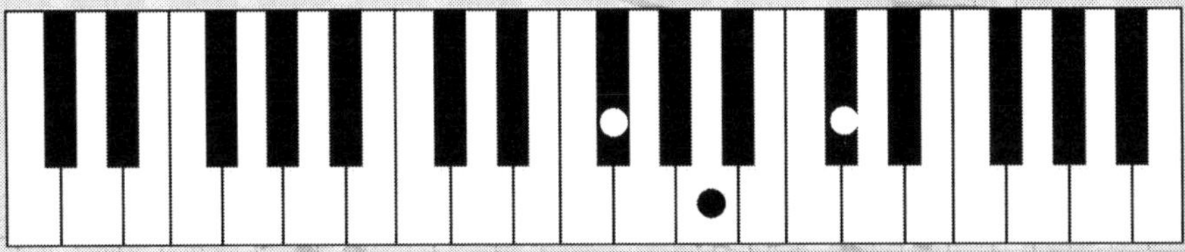
- F#/Gb 7 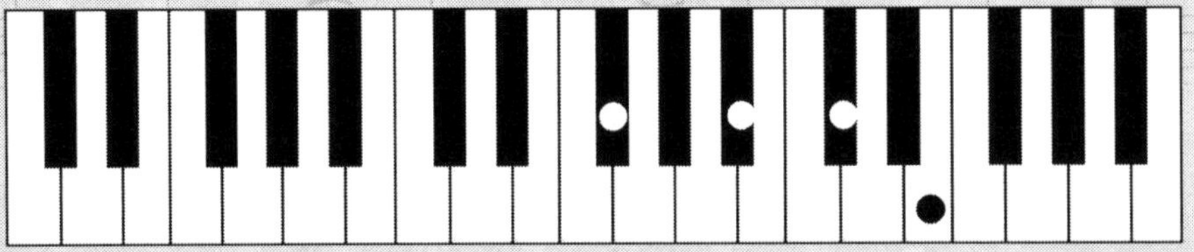
- F#/Gb maj7 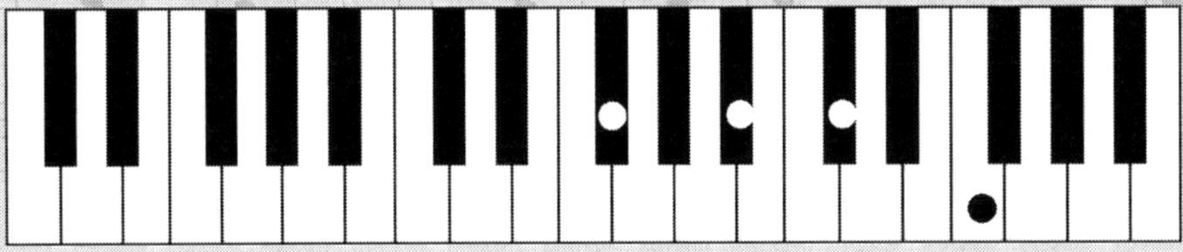
- F#/Gb min7 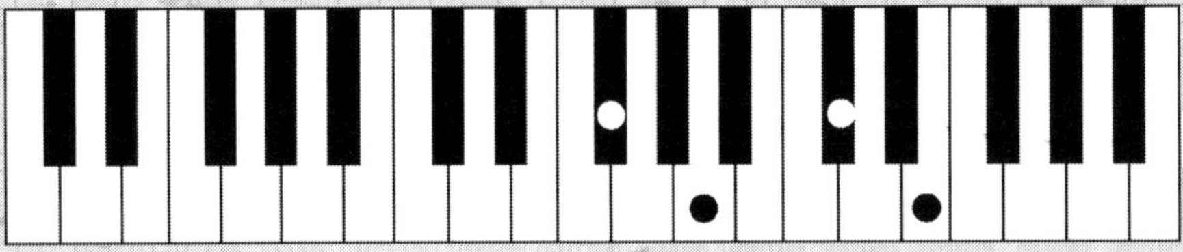
- F#/Gb sus4 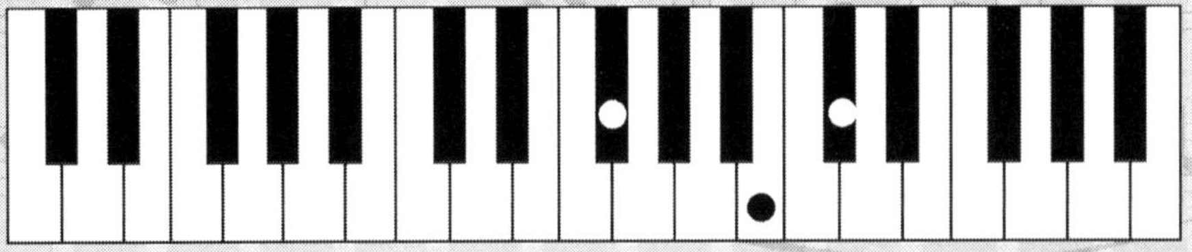
- F#/Gb sus2

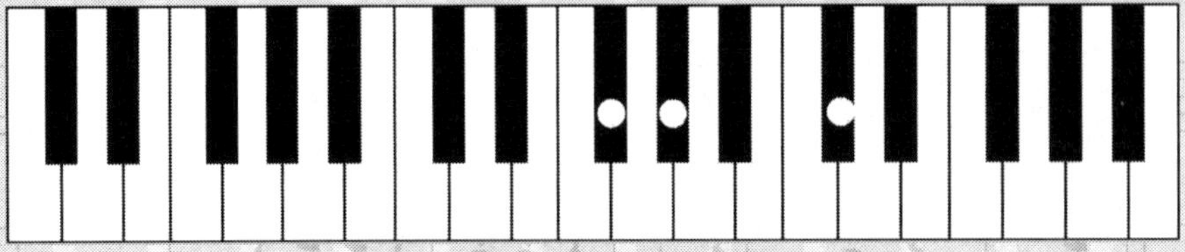

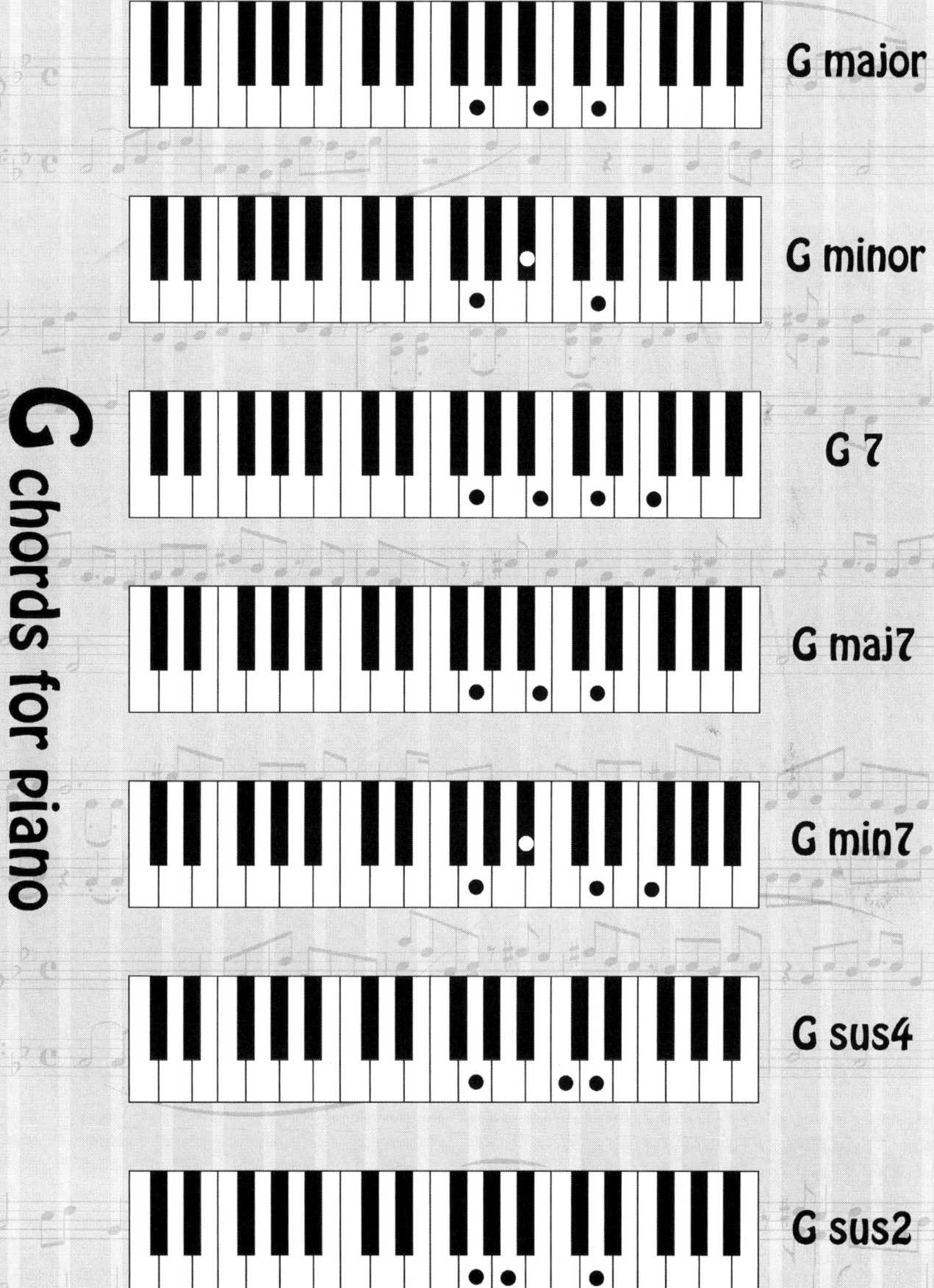

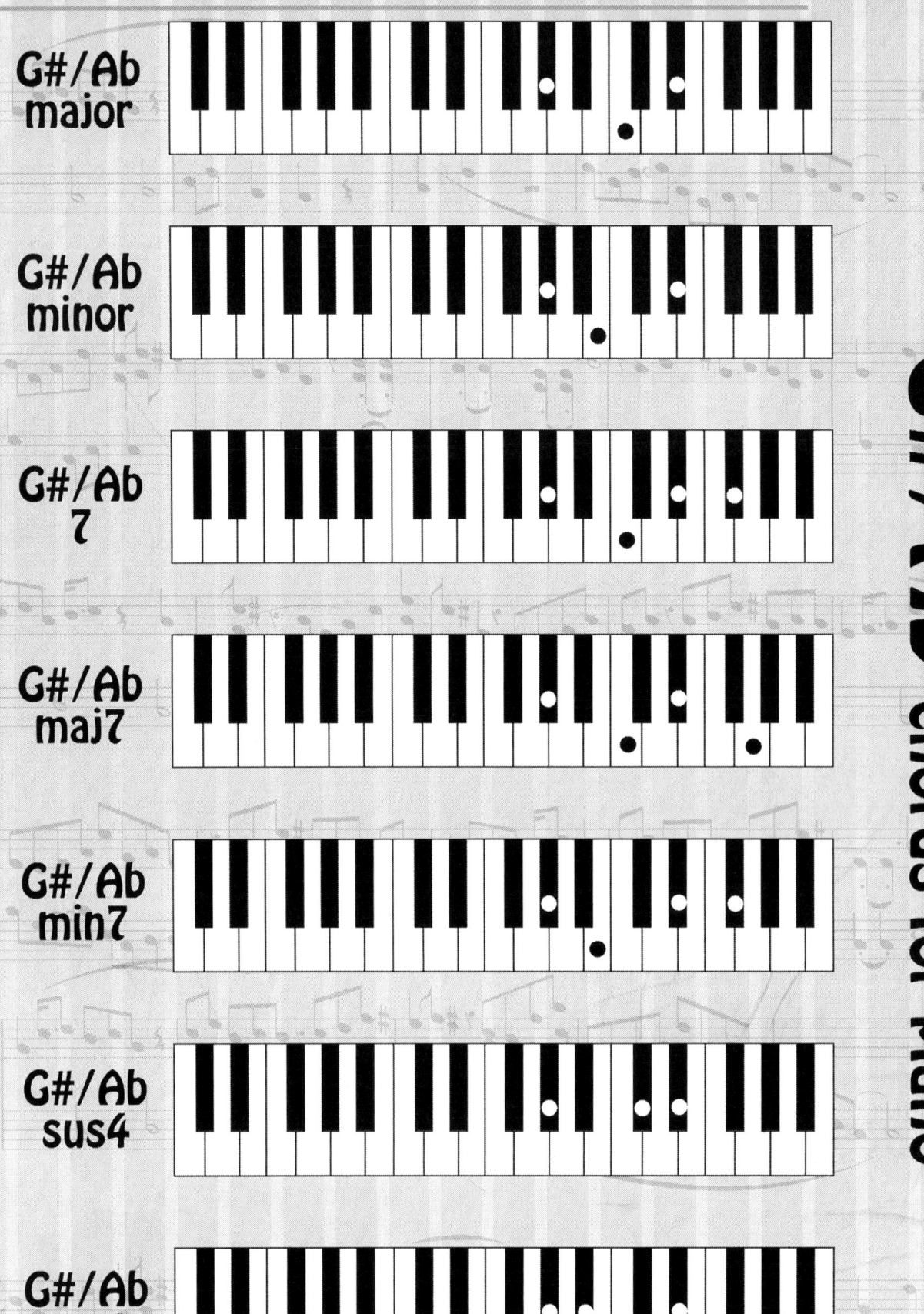

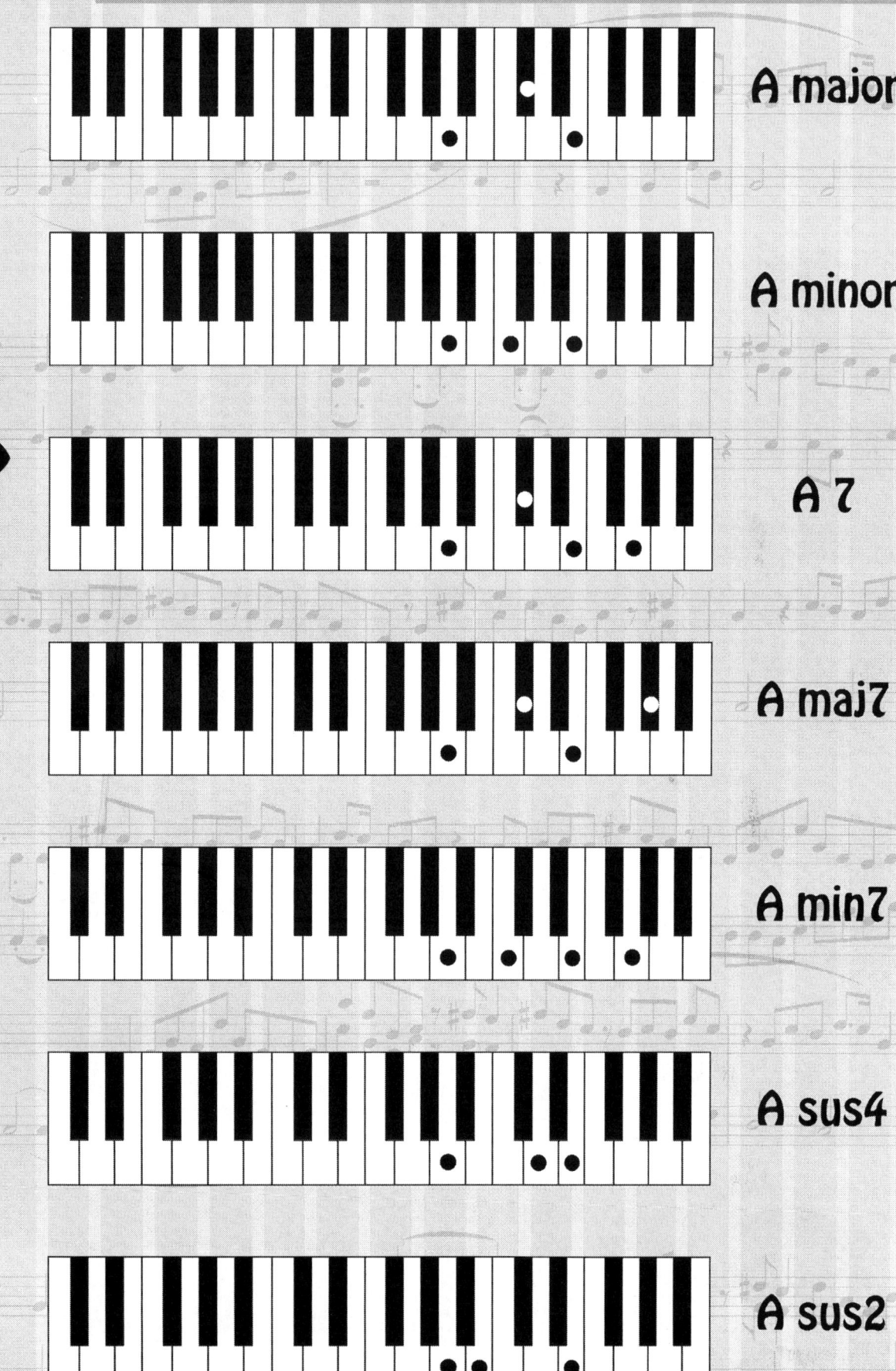

A#/Bb chords for piano

- A#/Bb major 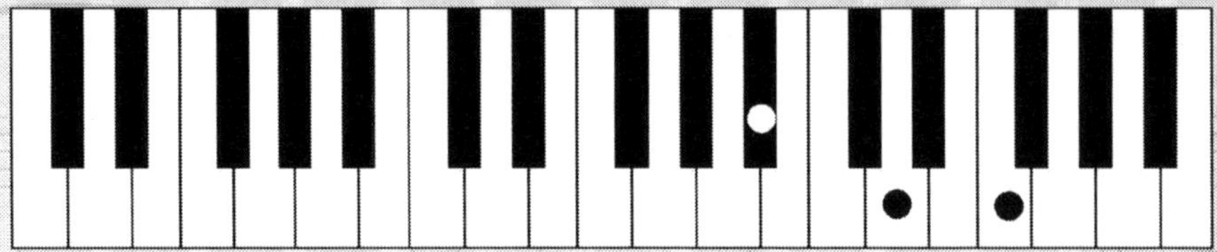
- A#/Bb minor 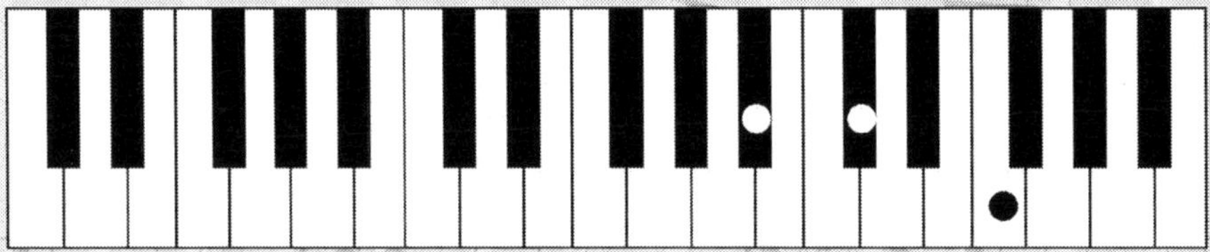
- A#/Bb 7 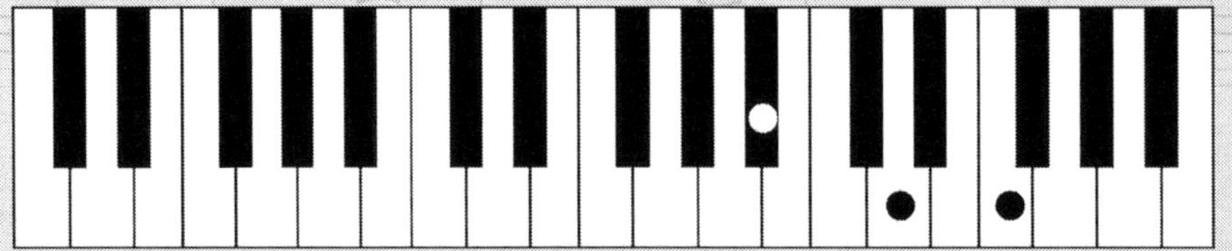
- A#/Bb maj7 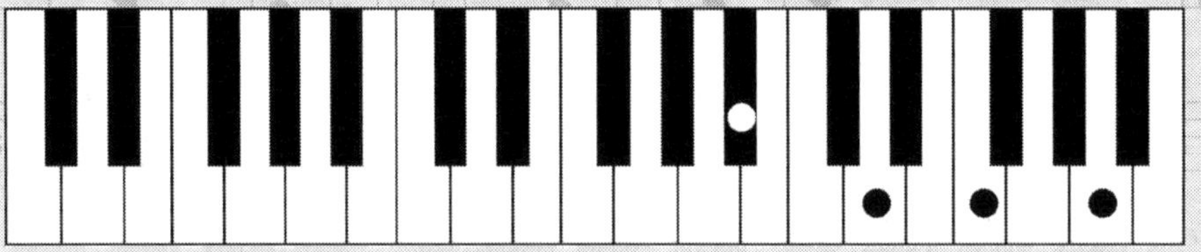
- A#/Bb min7 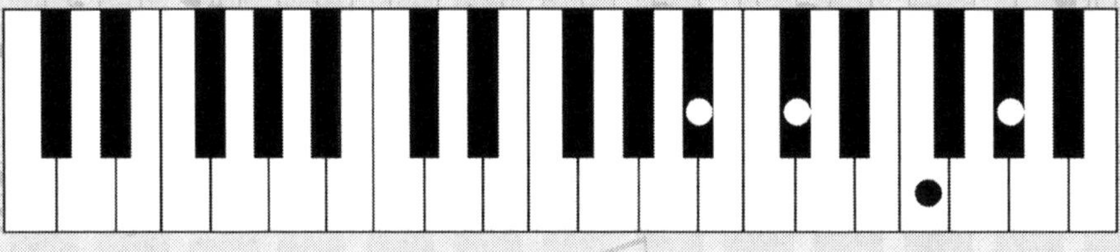
- A#/Bb sus4 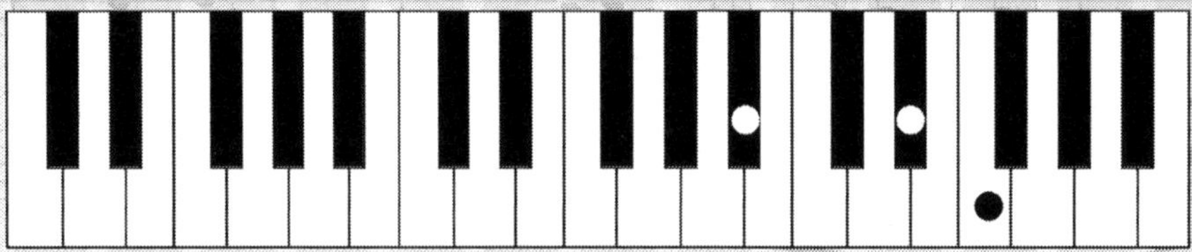
- A#/Bb sus2

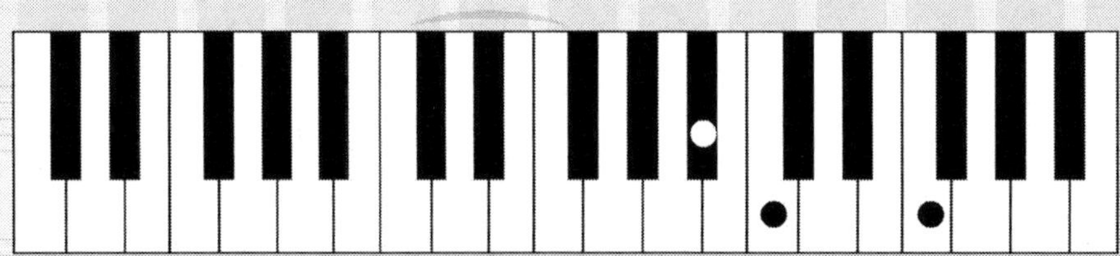

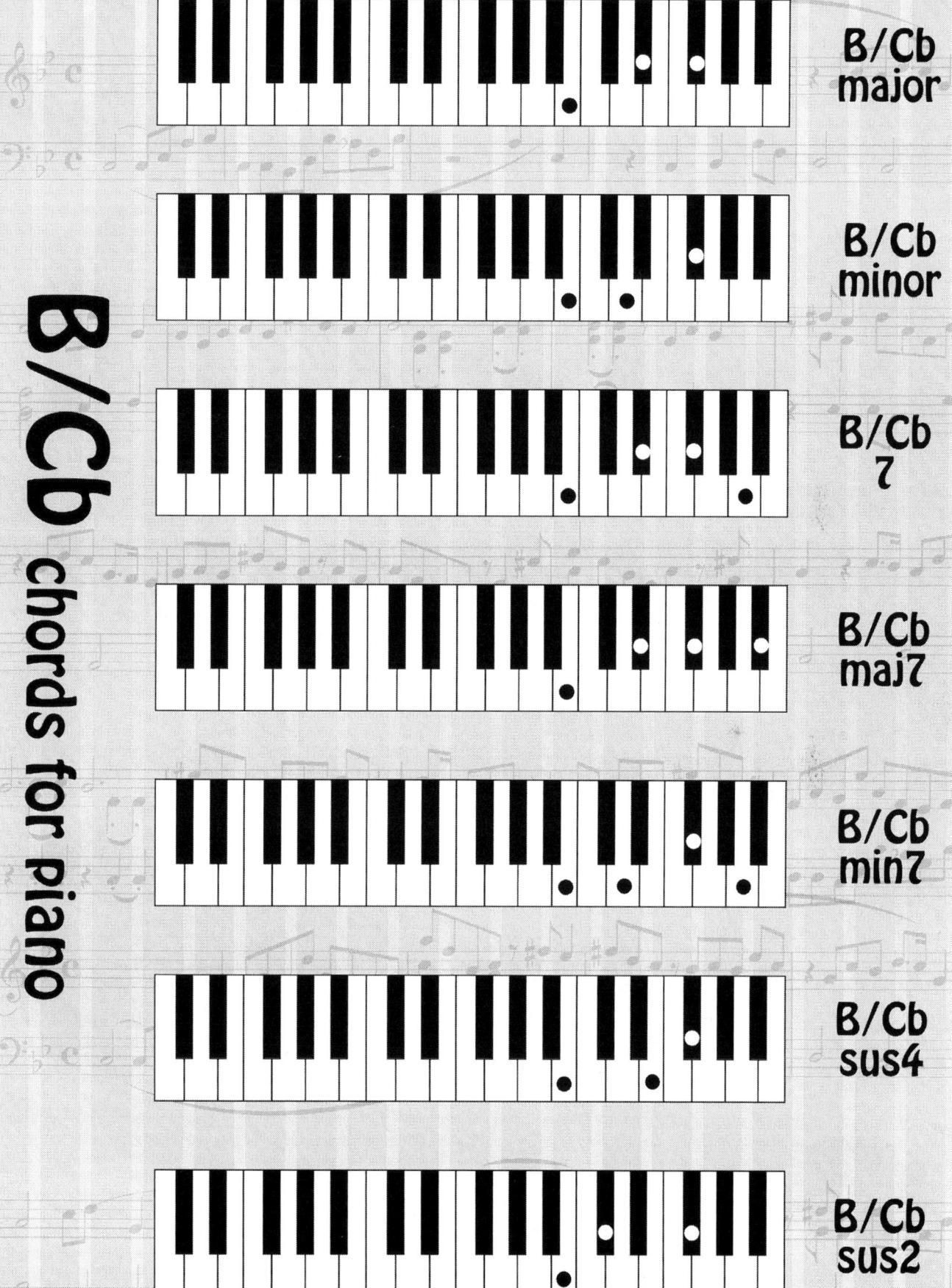

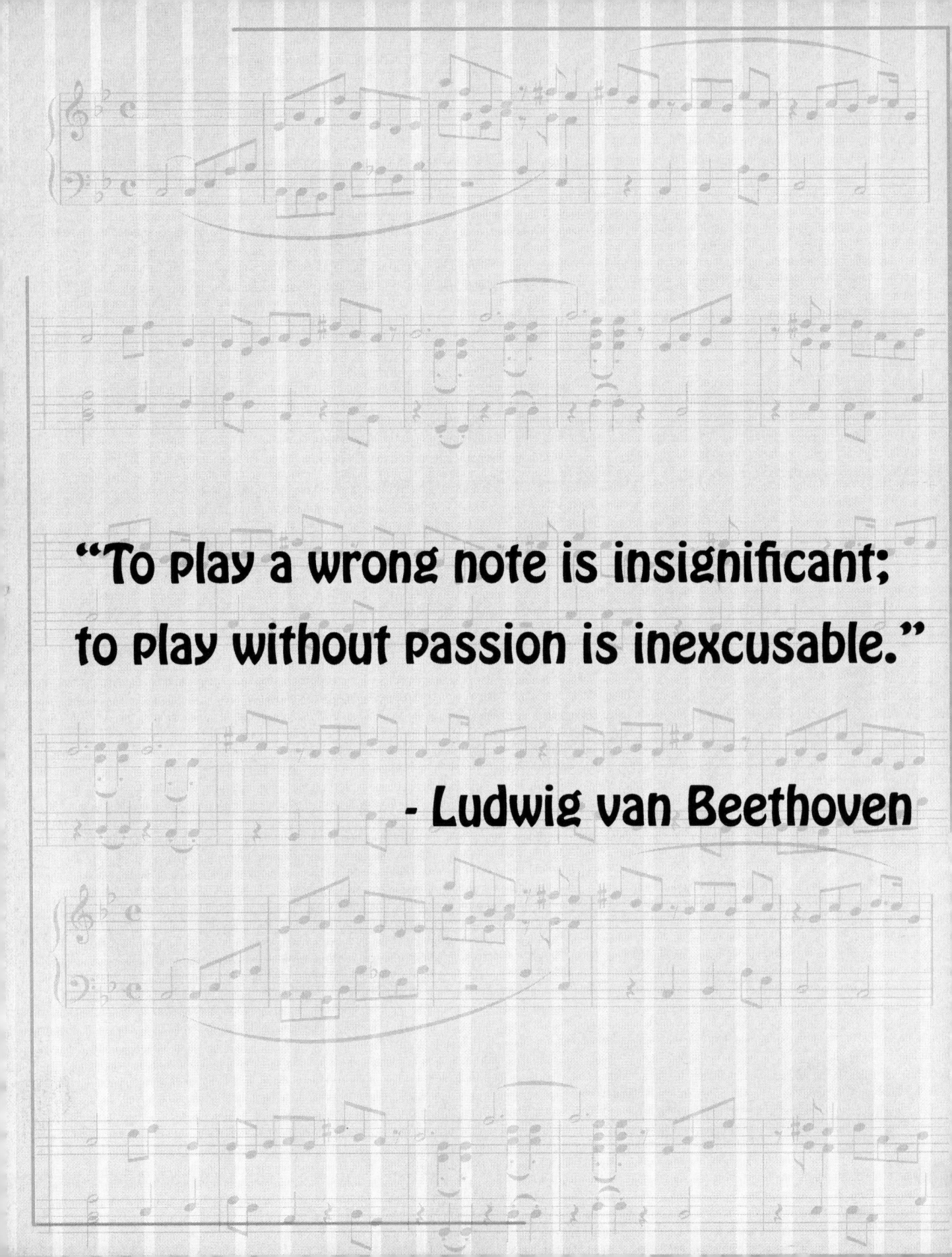

We hope you have enjoyed our
Piano Music Manuscript book
as much as we enjoyed working on
it. If so, please leave a review in
our book's page on the Amazon
website. This helps us to make
even better books for you.
Thank you for your support and
learning music with us!

www.bookcreators.net
www.twitter.com/bookcreators
www.facebook.com/bookcreators
www.instagram.com/welovemakingbooks

Printed in Great Britain
by Amazon